Classical GREECE

Published by

UNIVERSITY SCHOOL

at The University of Tulsa

TULSA, OKLAHOMA

ISBN Number: 1-893413-00-4

Manufactured in the United States of America

All proceeds from this series go to University School at The University of Tulsa,
a non-profit educational organization.

SAILS titles include:
> *Classical Greece*
> *Ancient Rome*
> *The Renaissance*
> *Baroque & Rococo*
> *Neoclassicism*
> *Romanticism*
> *Ancient Egypt*
> *Middle Ages*

Other books are in the planning phase. Additional information is available about SAILS materials
and University School.

Contact: University School at The University of Tulsa
> 800 South Tucker Avenue, Tulsa, Oklahoma 74104
> Phone: 918-631-5060   Fax: 918-631-5065
> Visit: 326 South College Avenue, Tulsa, Oklahoma 74104
> e-mail: debra-price@utulsa.edu

The University of Tulsa is an equal opportunity/affirmative action institution. For EEO/
AA information, contact the Office of Legal Compliance at (918) 631-2423, for disability
accommodations, contact Dr. Jane Corso at (918) 631-2315.

The SAILS Curriculum concept and ideas were developed in conjunction with a grant from the
U.S. Department of Education, Javits Gifted and Talented Students Education Grants Program;
Award Number R206A990007 for the period January 1999 through January 2003; in the amount
of $645,000.

Acknowledgements

Many thanks to Susan Coman and her staff at Protype Inc., Tulsa, Oklahoma,
who produced the series. Also thanks to copy editors Katie Abercrombie, Robyn
Bowman, Ekta Gupta, Kim Harper, and Andrea Sharrer for the countless hours
donated to this project.

Artwork courtesy of Photodisc, Artchives, clip art, and Patricia Hollingworth. Any
omission of acknowledgement is unintentional.

Preface

University School teachers created SAILS for students of all ages. SAILS is based on active interdisciplinary learning in a content-rich environment as used at University School. University School at The University of Tulsa is a school for gifted children from preschool through eighth grade. The active interdisciplinary learning approach presented in SAILS enables gifted behaviors to emerge in students in both regular and special classrooms.

The purpose of SAILS is to provide a framework for understanding historical patterns which is often omitted in world, national, and art history courses. This framework is developed by showing modern day links to ancient Western civilizations, presenting reccurring patterns in history, and acquiring an understanding of the basic ideals of these cultures. Every community in America has visual reminders of ancient civilizations which go unrecognized. Students of all ages can learn to recognize and appreciate this heritage.

SAILS was created by

Editor and Illustrator - Patricia L. Hollingsworth, Ed.D.

Writers and Teachers

Katie Abercrombie	Marilyn Howard
Sharon Block	Cyndie Kidwell
Debi Foster	Gina Lewis
Cathy Freeman	Alicia Parent
Kim Harper	Marti Sudduth

Patricia Hollingsworth

Contents

OLYMPICS

PHILOSOPHY

SCIENCE

REVIEW

BIBLIOGRAPHY / 87

This timeline is a simplified version of time periods. The dates are all approximate and in reality overlap with one another. One country may be starting a time period just as another is ending it. The idea is to provide some guidelines for understanding ideas and influences.

800BC-350AD	350-1350AD	1350-1600AD
CLASSICAL • GREEK • ROMAN	MEDIEVAL/MIDDLE AGES • ROMANESQUE • GOTHIC	RENAISSANCE

IDEALS

- **Classical Greek Ideals:**
  Freedom
  Symmetry
  Balance
  Beauty
  Order
  Dignity
  "Nothing to excess"

- **Classical Roman Ideals:**
  Grandeur
  Power
  Efficiency
  Practicality

- Life is short, difficult
- God all important
- Afterlife all important

- **Classical Ideals Revived:**
  God and humans important
  Harmony
  Balance
  Beauty
  Order
  Grandeur
  Power

ARCHITECTURE

- **Greek Classical:**
  Parthenon
  Balance, harmony, order

- **Roman Classical:**
  Pantheon
  Technology advancements

- **Romanesque:**
  Fortress-like

- **Gothic:**
  God-like proportion
  Light, airy
  Spires point to God

- **Renaissance Classical:**
  Symmetrical
  Built for God and humans
  Human proportions
  Solid

ART

- **Greeks: Idealistic**
  Classical ideals
- **Romans: Realistic**
  Mythological and
    human subjects
  Classical ideals

- Stiff, heavily draped sculpture
- Cartoon-like drawings
- Biblical subjects only

- Natural and realistic
- Balanced between repose
  and action
- Biblical, mythological, and
  human subjects

TIME LINE

1600-1750AD	1750-1800AD	1800-1850AD
• BAROQUE • ROCOCO	NEOCLASSICAL	ROMANTIC

IDEALS

- **Baroque**
  Emotion
  Grandeur
  Energy

- **Rococo**
  Enjoyment
  Pleasure

- **Classical Ideals Revived:**
  Freedom
  Dignity
  Balance
  Beauty
  Order

- Emotion
- Imagination
- Freedom
- Energy
- Turbulence

ARCHITECTURE

- **Versailles:**
  Elaborate
  Grand
- **Palaces:**
  Ornate
  Gold leaf
  Curlicues

- **Monticello:**
  Symmetry
  Balance
  Solid

- **Parliament Houses:**
  Gothic and Medieval

ART

- **Baroque:**
  Emotional
  Swirling
  Dramatic Subject Lighting
- **Rococo:**
  Pretty and Pleasant

- **Classical Ideals:**
  Balance
  Harmony
  Dignity

- Emotional
- Swirling
- Dramatic and exotic
  Lighting
  Subjects

7

Classical GREECE

Welcome to Classical Greece

Aristotle

My name is Aristotle. I am a Greek philosopher. I was asked to visit you today because my teacher, Plato, was too busy seeking truth and beauty. When I am as famous as Plato, I probably will not do these tours either.

Let me see now, my subject today is the building called the Parthenon. It is a Greek temple, something like your church or synagogue. However, we do not go inside to worship; we stand outside. We like simple shapes, and so we used a triangular shape, called a pediment, to hold up the roof of this temple. The pediment is held up by eight tall, elegant, Doric columns. It has been called the perfect building, even though it only took five years to build and does not have a single straight line. The lines were built to appear straight.

We Greeks like simple shapes, but we love to decorate the pediment with statues and paint them bright colors. The paint has worn off, and most of the sculpture has been taken away to museums, which really irks me. But where was I? Oh yes, the Parthenon was built to honor the Greek goddess Athena, the goddess of wisdom. The Parthenon was built on the Acropolis, which is a hill with other temples on it, in my city of Athens in Greece. The proportions of the Parthenon were determined by using the Golden Mean.

The building was approximately 235 feet long, 109 feet wide, and 60 feet tall. The triangular portion that held the roof is called the pediment. Oh, I told you that already. Anything else? Yes, the Parthenon is made of marble.

Pediment

Parthenon

Before I return to my work in Athens, I must explain this idea of classical. At times classical and ancient are used interchangeably. So a person might say classical Rome or ancient Rome and mean the same thing. When the term is classical Greece, I like to think that it means the most excellent example, the most marvelous model, a paragon of virtue. However, I realize that perhaps I am only seeing this from my point of view. This reminds me that I must return to study in Athens where I can continue to think with Plato about how we can know the truth.

Acropolis

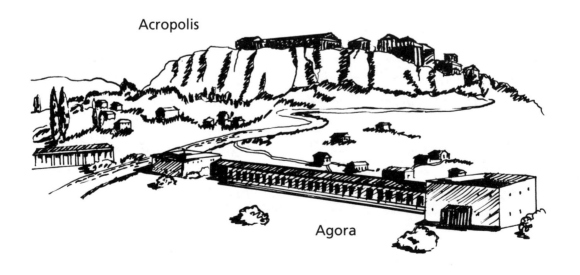

Agora

QUESTIONS ABOUT CLASSICAL GREECE

1. Who was Aristotle? _____

2. Who was his teacher? _____

3. What is the name of the famous Greek temple in Athens dedicated to

   Athena? _____

4. What is the Acropolis? _____

5. Who was Athena? _____

6. The triangular shape on the Parthenon and other buildings is

   called the _____ .

7. Sometimes classical and ancient mean the same thing. Other times classical

   means _____ .

8. Where did people worship in an ancient Greek temple? _____

9. The Parthenon was made of _____

   and had _____ (number of) columns.

10. What style were the columns? _____

GREECE

WORD**BOX**

outside	eight	high city
pediment	Doric	excellent
goddess of wisdom	Plato	Parthenon
philosopher		

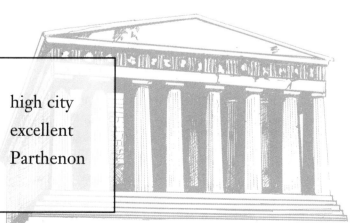

GREECE
QUICK FACTS

DATES: 800 BC–100 AD

Homer

Dates for time periods are approximate. They vary widely depending upon what is included. The 800 BC–100 AD period includes the first Olympic games and stretches into the Roman era.

800-700 BC	Homer's *Iliad* and *Odyssey*
776 BC	Olympic Games
479-431 BC	Golden Age of Pericles
447-442 BC	Parthenon built
431-404 BC	Peloponnesian War, headed by Sparta
404 BC	Sparta defeated Athens
356-323 BC	Alexander the Great, ruler of Greece, conquers Egypt, and all land from Greece to India
146 BC	Rome conquers Greece
100 AD	Greece part of Roman Empire

VALUES & IDEALS

Golden Mean—"Nothing to excess"
Balance, order, harmony
Human dignity, individuality, and freedom
Living a life balanced between the body and the mind
Rational inquiry—a search for order within nature's complexity

Pericles

GOVERNMENT

Small democratic city states
Adult male landowners voted

FOREMOST CITY

Athens

TYPICAL CITY-STATE LAYOUT

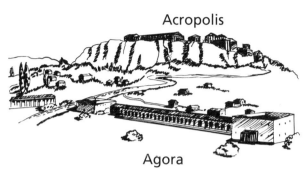

Acropolis

Agora

An *Acropolis* (high city) was a combination fortress and worship place on a hill. The *agora* (marketplace), with a shady *stoa* (porch) as a meeting place, sat at the foot of the hill. Homes and farms surrounded the *agora*.

PROFESSIONS

Craftsmen and tradesmen

FAMOUS PEOPLE

Pericles	Athenian leader during height of classical building program
Socrates	Greek philosopher
Plato	Philosopher who believed physical world only pale reflection of true reality and understanding comes through reason
Aristotle	Studied the physical world
	Conducted extensive classification of animals and plants
	The father of life sciences and the scientific method
Euclid	Mathematician
Praxiteles	Sculptor of *Venus de Medici*
Myron	Sculptor of *Discus Thrower*

ART

Idealized figures exemplified harmony and order

S-curve sculpture—weight on one leg gave feeling of frozen movement

Human body expressed human spirit, individuality

Human body was natural and beautiful

Idealized human body was to reflect the Golden Mean

SCIENCE

coin

All of these dates are approximate.

700 BC	Greek coins created
550 BC	Math and geometry theories of Pythagoras
510 BC	Map making developed
400 BC	Crossbow catapults for warfare
287–212 BC	Archimedes, mathematician and scientist, invented the water screw to lift water
50 AD	Hero, Greek inventor, created a steam machine

ARCHITECTURE

Parthenon

Parthenon:
- Built in only five years, 447-442 BC by Ictinus and Callicrates
- Built without mortar
- Stayed intact until 1687 AD when hit by cannon fire during a war
- Phidias, sculptor of pediments and metopes on frieze
- Used eye-pleasing optical illusions (lines look straight but actually bowed)
- Made of marble
- Eight Doric columns
- Columns, stacked slices of stone with a plug to keep them in line

Greek temple

Other Greek Temples
- Also represented symmetry, harmony, and order
- Doric columns used mostly in Greece, Ionic in other Greek settlements in Asia, Corinthian columns used in Rome

column

ENTERTAINMENT

Amphitheaters, built for Greek drama
Olympic Games—helped unite Greeks, held in
Olympia for 1,000 years starting in 776 BC

Greek amphitheater

GREEK TRIVIA

1. Name the most famous classical Greek temple: _____

2. Name two famous Greek scientists:

   _____

   _____

3. List three ancient Greek philosophers:

   _____

   _____

   _____

4. Name four scientific discoveries or inventions:

   _____   _____

   _____   _____

5. List five classical Greek ideals:

   _____   _____

   _____   _____

   _____

IDEALS

PERICLES

Pericles was determined to rebuild and protect Athens after it was destroyed during the war with the Persians. Great walls over four miles long were built from Athens to the harbor where a new port city was built. Hippodamus laid out the city with straight streets in a precise geometric pattern, like some streets are planned today. The old city streets had a random plan which they hoped would confuse any enemy who came to the city.

Pericles

Activity~

Draw your own city streets here. Make one plan geometric and symmetric, and another plan more random.

Geometric Plan

Random Plan

Which plan makes it easier to figure out how to move from one place to the other? What would happen in each plan if there was a fire?

GREEK IDEALS: SYMMETRY, ORDER, BALANCE, HARMONY

Greek art, architecture, and life were to reflect symmetry, order, simplicity, balance, and harmony. The Golden Mean was the ideal. It meant "nothing to excess." Here are some examples from Greek life.

IDEALS

Discus Thrower

Parthenon

Greek tunic or peplos

SYMMETRY is often seen in nature and in human creations. Symmetrical means that the sides match. They are mirror images of each other.

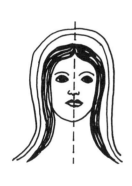

human face

animal body

tree

Draw some of your own examples of symmetry.

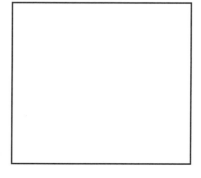

ASYMMETRY is also seen in nature and in human creations. Asymmetrical means the sides are different. If the object was folded in the middle, the sides would not match.

tree

building

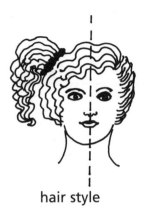

hair style

Draw some of your own examples of asymmetry.

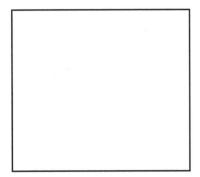

ORDER is arranging things in a deliberate, thoughtful way.

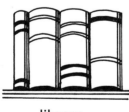

library

shell collection

Draw some of your own examples of order.

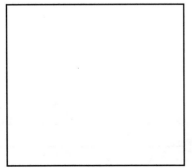

DISORDER is the result of no particular plan or thought to the arrangement.

trash

shells on a beach

IDEALS

Draw some of your own examples of disorder.

SIMPLICITY is uncomplicated, streamlined, reduced to basic essentials.

periwinkle

pearl

pencil

Draw some of your own examples of simplicity.

COMPLEXITY describes things made up of many parts or facets.

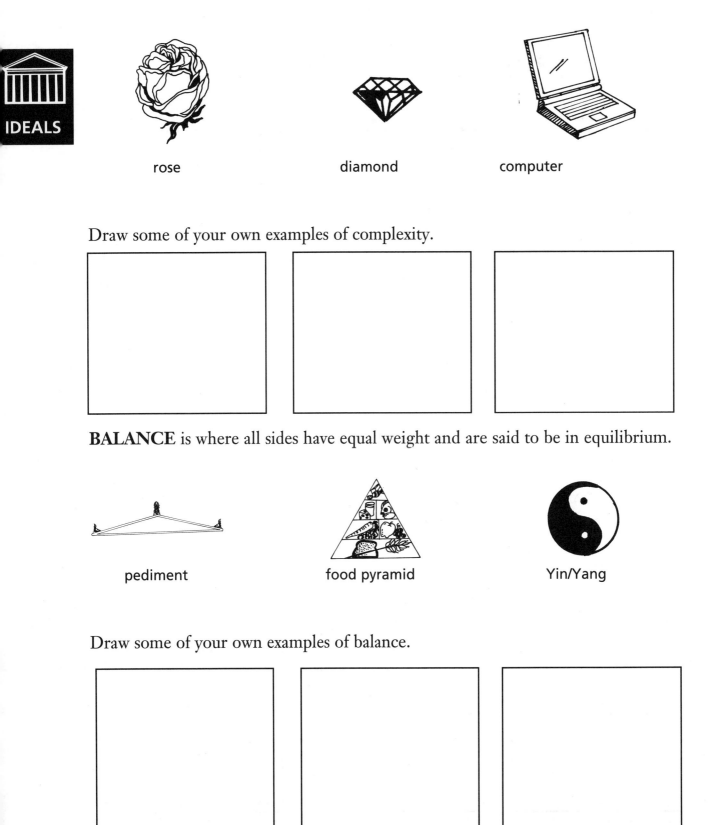

rose

diamond

computer

Draw some of your own examples of complexity.

BALANCE is where all sides have equal weight and are said to be in equilibrium.

pediment

food pyramid

Yin/Yang

Draw some of your own examples of balance.

UNBALANCED is when a part or side is missing or larger than others.

one-hinged door

junk food

fan with broken blade

Draw some things of your own that are unbalanced.

HARMONY is when everything comes together to make a pleasing whole.

song

peace

Draw some of your own examples of harmony.

DISCORD is the lack of agreement or harmony.

noise

war

Draw some of your own examples of discord.

Make a list of Greek ideals.   *What is the opposite?*

THE PARTHENON: Symmetry, Order, Balance, Harmony

The Parthenon in Athens had balance and harmony between natural forms (people and animals) on the pediments and metopes on the frieze and more geometric forms on the columns, steps, roof, and pediment.

Built from 447–442 BC

There was also balance between the white marble of the geometric forms and the colorfully painted people and animals. Try out your own color scheme on the Parthenon.

Create your own pediment designs.

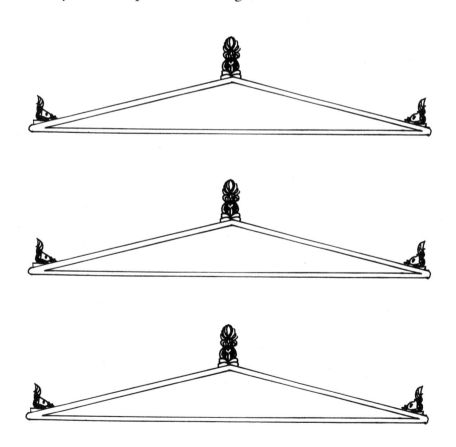

PARTHENON ANALOGIES

IDEALS

The Parthenon in Athens was built to express the ideals of the Greek people. It was both a fortress, if needed, and a place of worship high on a hilltop called an *acropolis*. The Parthenon was made of delicate white marble with elegant, colorful sculptures on the pediments and metopes.

Fill in answers below to compare one thing to another. Use the IDEA Box for analogy ideas or create your own ideas if you wish.

Parthenon on the Acropolis

EXAMPLE: The Parthenon is as symmetrical as a beautiful face.

The Parthenon is as harmonious as _____ .

The Parthenon is as orderly as _____ .

The Parthenon is as symmetrical as _____ .

The Parthenon is as simple as _____ .

The Parthenon is as balanced as _____ .

The tall, white, fluted columns are as harmonious as _____ .

The tall, white, fluted columns are as orderly as _____ .

The tall, white, fluted columns are as symmetrical as _____ .

The tall, white, fluted columns are as simple as _____ .

The tall, white, fluted columns are as balanced as _____ .

GREECE: **PARTHENON**

IDEA BOX

Use any of these you wish or create your own.

- fir trees
- a box of pencils
- a choir
- crisp, pleated drapes
- a gymnast
- louvers of a door
- a pair of swans
- spokes of a wheel
- the queen's garden
- a keyboard
- a flight of geese
- packages of paper
- window shutters
- marching bands
- piano keys
- a white lily

Write a paragraph about the Parthenon using the analogies you created.

_____

_____

_____

_____

_____

COLUMNS

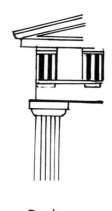

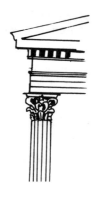

Doric   Ionic   Corinthian

Greeks used mostly Doric columns. Greek colonies used Ionic columns. Romans used all three types. Columns shaped like women are called caryatids (kar-ee-`at-ids).

Activity~

- Use your body to show each of the three types of columns.
- Create some of your own types of columns and name them.

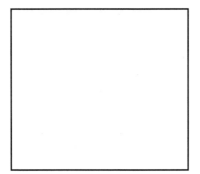

PARTHENON DESCRIPTIONS

The Parthenon housed a huge 40-foot statue of Athena, daughter of Zeus, and the treasures and offerings brought to the gods and goddesses. The gold and ivory statue of Athena could be seen from outside the building where worship took place.

Make a list of many, varied, and unusual single words to describe the Parthenon. Use any words from the IDEA BOX that you wish or create your own.

_____

_____

_____

_____

_____

_____

_____

_____

_____

_____

GREECE: PARTHENON

IDEA BOX

Use these words if they express what you feel about the building.

- orderly
- oneness
- unity
- symmetry
- peaceful

- sensible
- simplicity
- clear
- direct
- powerful

- logical
- balanced
- stable
- steady
- rational

Diamanté Poem

IDEALS

The classical Greeks believed in balance, order, and harmony.

A diamanté (dee-a-mon-`tay) poem is completely balanced because the first half is completely identical to the second half. Study the structure of a diamanté poem below.

Study the drawing on the Greek vase of the women dressed in their ancient style of clothing. Write a diamanté poem describing them.

1. topic _____

2. two describing words _____ _____
   (adjectives)

3. three action words _____ _____ _____
   (verbs)

4. one group of words _____

5. three action words _____ _____ _____
   (verbs)

6. two describing words _____ _____
   (adjectives)

7. renaming word _____
   (synonym)

Aesop's Fables

IDEALS

Do you remember the story of "The Tortoise and the Hare?" It is about a very slow but non-stopping tortoise and a fast but easily distracted rabbit (hare). The two decide to race, but in the middle of the race the rabbit decides to take a nap because he is very far ahead and is sure that he will win. The tortoise keeps plodding along, passes the sleeping rabbit, and wins the race.

This story was written about 2,500 years ago! Can you imagine how old that is? The writer is thought to be an ancient Greek slave called Aesop. He wrote a lot of stories, and they all had a moral or a lesson to be learned from the story. The moral of the tortoise and hare story above is that persistence (never giving up) is more important than speed.

Draw a picture that shows what happened in "The Tortoise and the Hare."

Pretend that you are the tortoise. Write 5 words to describe how you feel.

_____ _____ _____ _____ _____

Now pretend that you are the hare and write 5 more words.

_____ _____ _____ _____ _____

Write Your Own Aesop's Fable

IDEALS

Read several of Aesop's fables to become familiar with the style.

Remember that each of his fables ended with a moral lesson or advice.
Aesop always had a point to make with each story. Decide upon the moral for your story first and place it on the line labeled "moral" on the next page.

You can pick a moral from Aesop's list or choose your own:

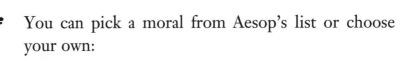

- A fish in the hand is worth two in the sea.
- Beauty is in the eye of the beholder.
- Our own home always seems best to us.
- Sometimes the weak can help the strong.

Now you need to pick the characters for your story. Most of Aesop's characters were animals, so choose two animals and draw their pictures in the box below.

Now write your story. Start on this sheet and continue on another sheet of paper if needed.

IDEALS

_____

_____

_____

_____

_____

_____

_____

_____

_____

_____

_____

Moral:

_____

_____

_____

SPARTAN MILITARY CODES

WAR

The rulers of Sparta, the Greek city-state that conquered Athens in 404 BC, developed a way of sending special messages to their military commanders in the field. The Spartan leader would take two wooden dowels that were exactly alike. The leader kept one and the military commander would keep the other. When a message was to be sent, the dowel would be wrapped entirely with a long narrow strip of parchment with no empty spaces. The message would be written down the stick with one letter on each ribbon of paper. When the strip of parchment was removed, the letters appeared mixed up. Only when the parchment was wrapped around the dowel of the same length and size did the message reappear.

Make a list of secret messages that you might wish to send.

_____

_____

_____

_____

_____

_____

_____

_____

MAKE YOUR OWN CODED MESSAGES

You will need:
- 2 identical dowels (same width and length)
- narrow strips of paper, attached together into a long strip
- tape
- pen or pencil

WAR

Keep one dowel for yourself and give another to a friend to whom you want to send your secret message.

Tape the end of your long strip of paper to the end of your dowel. Wrap (don't tape) the strip of paper around your dowel. Be careful not to leave any empty spaces as you wind.

Write your message down the side of the dowel, one letter on each ribbon down and on all sides of the dowel.

1. Carefully remove the strip of paper and roll it up.
2. Give it to your friend and see if he or she can read your secret message.

SHIPS FOR WAR AND PEACE

The Greeks were great shipbuilders and mapmakers. King Heron ordered a three-masted ship be built to transport soldiers, grain, or royalty. It was a combination freight ship, warship, and royal yacht. It was operated by a crew of thousands and decorated with stories of the *Iliad*.

WAR

Activity~

MAKE YOUR OWN SHIP

Materials:
- Anything that floats — milk cartons, detergent bottles, popsicle sticks.

- Try using different materials for sails.

- Attach your masts with clay, Play-Doh™, etc.

How many sails can your ship handle? Does having three masts help? How? Any problems? How will the wind affect your ship's handling ability?

Draw a picture of your best design.

EDUCATION FOR WAR AND PEACE

THE *ILIAD* AND THE *ODYSSEY*

WAR

The Greeks spent time and energy discussing and thinking about the kind of society they wanted. They believed that people should live a balanced life with nothing to excess. They believed that people should develop both their minds and their bodies. The Greeks believed in freedom, the importance of the individual, and in creative thought.

Formal education for boys included learning to be good warriors as well as being peaceful, thoughtful citizens. Students had to memorize long passages from Homer's *Iliad* and *Odyssey*. They also developed their bodies for times of war.

The *Iliad* and the *Odyssey* are a group of stories that tell what happened before and after the Trojan wars. They tell about the idealism and the tragedy of war. The legend is that the Trojan wars started because the Trojans stole Helen, a beautiful and greatly loved Greek maiden.

1. Do you think that was a good or bad reason for the Greeks to go to war? Write your reasons.

_____

_____

_____

2. Why do you think countries go to war? Use the IDEA BOX on the next page or write your own ideas.

_____

_____

_____

GREECE

WAR

IDEA **BOX**

- To protect their land.
- To protect their people.
- To get more land and wealth.
- The leader decides to have war.
- To make the country more powerful.
- Hatred of the enemy.
- To fight for ideas or beliefs.

3. Why do wars usually stop? Use the IDEA BOX or write your own ideas.

_____

_____

_____

GREECE

IDEA **BOX**

- One country is the clear winner.
- Each side loses many lives.
- War seems like a bad way to solve problems.
- Everyone is tired of war.
- A few groups get together to start peace talks.

GREEK SUPERHEROES

The Greeks wanted their young men to think carefully before choosing war as a solution to problems. The epic poems of Homer, handed down from generation to generation, were meant to help the Greeks learn from their past mistakes. What follows are stories about two Greek heroes Achilles and Ulysses.

LEGENDS

> **USE YOUR IMAGINATION:** These stories can be the basis for plays that you can create by yourself or with your friends.
>
> **FACT AND FICTION.** Some stories are true stories based entirely on facts. Other stories, such as *The Three Bears*, are fiction. They did not really happen. Legends, like the stories about Achilles and Ulysses, are based on a combination of fact and fiction.

Achilles' Heel

Long ago, in a place called Greece, lived a lovely young woman named Thetis. She was a sea nymph, which means she guarded the sea. She was married to a king. When Thetis gave birth to a son, she named him Achilles.

> **USE YOUR IMAGINATION:** *Come and sit on my lap. I will rock you like Thetis used to rock Achilles.*

Thetis loved her son, Achilles, very much. She wanted to protect him. She did not want anything bad to happen to him. She thought, "Maybe I can just hold him forever and ever. That way he will never get hurt." But Thetis grew tired of holding Achilles, and Achilles grew tired of being held.

"This is not going to work," she said. "But what should I do to protect my son?"

USE YOUR IMAGINATION: *Show me how you feel when I have been holding you for a long time.*

Finally Thetis, guardian of seas, oceans, and waters, remembered a magic river. Thetis had been told that a dip in the River Styx would protect one from harm. It was a long walk, but Thetis decided to take Achilles to the magic river.

USE YOUR IMAGINATION: *Let's pretend that we are going for a long walk to the magic river. It's such a long trip, we may have to pretend to stop to eat and sleep. Let me know when you are rested and we will continue our journey.*

When they arrived at the river, Thetis picked up Achilles and held him tightly by the heel. She gently dipped his whole body, head and all, into the magic River Styx. She talked to him as she dipped him into the water. "Do not be afraid little Achilles because this magic river is going to protect you."

Water covered every part of Achilles except the heel that Thetis was holding when she dipped him into the river. Achilles' heel was not protected. It was vulnerable, but no one would know this for many years.

LEGENDS

USE YOUR IMAGINATION: *Lie down, and I will pretend to dip you into the magic river. Do not be afraid. I will hold your heel tightly.*

Achilles grew to be a strong young man just at the time of the terrible Trojan War. All of the men in Greece were expected to go to war. Again Thetis worried. She believed that he was protected from harm because she had dipped him into the magic River Styx, but she didn't want to take chances.

USE YOUR IMAGINATION: *Squat down very low. Now pretend to be growing tall, like Achilles did. I will be Thetis and try to think of ways to protect you.*

Thetis thought to herself, "Since only men have been sent to this war, all that must be done is to make Achilles look like a woman."

So Thetis sent Achilles away to the palace of King Lycomedes, where he dressed to look like one of the king's daughters.

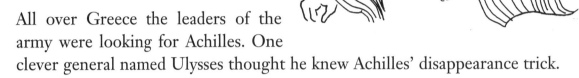

> **USE YOUR IMAGINATION:**
> *Pretend that you are Achilles dressing yourself to look like one of the king's daughters. Now off you go to the palace.*

LEGENDS

All over Greece the leaders of the army were looking for Achilles. One clever general named Ulysses thought he knew Achilles' disappearance trick.

General Ulysses disguised himself as a merchant, a seller of goods. He brought many beautiful dresses and just a few weapons used by the army to the king's palace. While King Lycomedes' daughters looked at the dresses, Achilles only looked at the weapons. Now Ulysses was sure he had found Achilles. Both Ulysses and Achilles took off their disguises.

Ulysses said, "Come Achilles. You and I will go to Troy and win this war." Achilles, who had always been interested in battle, was ready to fight the Trojans.

> **USE YOUR IMAGINATION:** *I will be Ulysses. I will disguise myself as a merchant and bring the dresses and weapons to the palace. You be Achilles and choose only to look at the weapons. As Ulysses, I will discover that you are Achilles. I will ask you to fight in the Trojan War.*

When Thetis learned that Achilles was going to war, she had Vulcan, also known as Hephaestus, make a special suit of armor for him. Vulcan was a superhero who had magical powers over fire and metal. The armor that Vulcan made for Achilles fit him perfectly. The shield was made of five layers of metal. The crest of the helmet was made of gold. Achilles wore this splendid armor each time he went into battle.

For years Achilles fought bravely and well. Then one day an enemy learned of Achilles' vulnerable heel. Paris, the son of the king of Troy, shot a poison arrow into Achilles' heel and killed him. Now when someone talks about an Achilles' heel, they mean something that is not protected, something that is vulnerable.

LEGENDS

> **USE YOUR IMAGINATION:** *You pretend to be Achilles putting on your armor to battle the Trojans. Now Paris shoots you in the heel, and you pretend to be dying.*

After Achilles' death, Thetis told the Greeks to give the armor to the bravest living warrior. Ulysses was given the splendid armor, which he used in many famous battles. One such battle involved a huge wooden horse. But that's another story.

> **USE YOUR IMAGINA-TION:** *You have been selected by the Greeks to present Ulysses with Achilles' splendid suit of armor. Make up a speech to tell Ulysses when you give him the armor.*

ACHILLES' QUESTIONS

1. Who was given Achilles' shield?

   _____

2. Greek stories often have a noble hero who has some tragic flaw.
   What was Achilles' flaw?

   _____

3. Today, when it is said that someone has an Achilles' heel, what does it
   mean?

   _____

4. What might be some tragic flaws in a person's character?

   _____

   _____

5. Write a paragraph about this person.

   _____

   _____

   _____

   _____

   _____

   _____

   _____

GREECE
IDEA BOX

- meanness
- short temper
- sharp tongue
- thoughtlessness
- impulsiveness
- impatience
- arrogance
- intolerance

Ulysses and the Trojan Horse

The war between the Greeks and the Trojans began when a beautiful Greek queen named Helen was stolen by Paris, a Trojan prince. The Greeks decided to fight to get Helen back. Greek soldiers sailed to Troy with General Achilles and General Ulysses, also known as Odysseus, the Wanderer.

LEGENDS

USE YOUR IMAGINATION: *I will pretend to be Paris and steal Helen. I will take her to Troy, which has high, thick walls on all sides of the city. You sail with General Ulysses and follow us to Troy.*

For nearly ten years, the Greeks had been fighting the Trojans. Achilles had been shot in the heel and killed by Paris. The Greek soldiers were becoming discouraged. Just as they were about to give up, General Ulysses had an idea that would win the war. "We will build a huge wooden horse," he decided.

USE YOUR IMAGINATION: *Pretend to be a tired Greek soldier. I will be General Ulysses and tell you my plan.*

43

The soldiers grumbled, "A wooden horse can't help us win the war." However, they obeyed Ulysses' orders. Then late one night, Ulysses ordered that the horse be quietly moved close to the walls of the city of Troy. There, Ulysses and most of the soldiers climbed into the horse where they could not be seen and did not make a sound.

LEGENDS

USE YOUR IMAGINATION: *You are a soldier building the huge wooden horse. Now drag the horse to the walls of the city of Troy. Climb inside the horse and sit quietly so the Trojans will not know you are there.*

The next part of Ulysses' plan was to make the Trojans think that the Greeks had given up and gone home. In the morning, the Trojans woke up and saw Greek ships sailing away. They began to shout, "The Greeks have given up and are sailing home!" They did not know that most of the ships were hidden in nearby islands.

USE YOUR IMAGINATION: *You are sailing a Greek ship away from Troy. I will be a Trojan, shouting, "The Greeks are leaving. They have given up." Now hide your ship on an island where I cannot see you.*

The Trojans were so delighted that the Greeks were gone that they ran out of the gates of the city. Just outside the city wall, they found the huge wooden horse. The people of Troy began to ask questions. "What is this thing that the Greeks have left behind? What is it for? Why did they leave it? What should we do with it?"

USE YOUR IMAGINATION: *Be a Trojan who has just come out of the city walls and found a huge wooden horse.*

LEGENDS

A wise man named Laocoön told the people to destroy the horse. He said, "I fear the Greeks even when they offer gifts." Then he threw his spear and hit the wooden horse. Inside the horse the Greeks could hear everything that was happening, but they did not make a sound.

USE YOUR IMAGINATION: *Pretend to be Laocoön. Throw your spear at the wooden horse.*

The next moment a Greek named Sinon was found by the Trojans. Sinon pretended to be angry with Ulysses. He said, "Because Ulysses left me here to die, I will tell you the secret of the wooden horse. The horse was made so large that it would not fit through your city gates. The Greeks knew if you were to get the horse inside the city walls, it would mean your victory. This horse was to be a gift to the powerful goddess Minerva. Whoever has the horse has the favor of Minerva."

Laocoön again tried to warn the Trojans about the horse, but no one was listening.

USE YOUR IMAGINATION: *Be Sinon as he is pretending to be angry with Ulysses. Tell the Trojans the "secret" of the horse that Ulysses told you to tell. Be careful not to tell the real secret.*

The people of Troy began to shout, "The horse belongs to us. Bring the Trojan horse into the city." But the gates of the city were too small to allow the huge horse to enter. "Tear down part of the wall. We must have our Trojan horse. It is our trophy for winning the war against the Greeks." So the Trojans tore down part of the wall that protected their city to make way for a wooden horse that would cause their downfall.

LEGENDS

USE YOUR IMAGINATION: *Help the Trojans tear down part of their city wall. Now drag the Trojan horse into the city.*

The Trojans spent the day and evening celebrating their victory over the Greeks. Finally everyone in the city slept, everyone except the Greeks. Ulysses and his men quietly slipped out of the horse. In a short time, the Greeks gained control of the city of Troy.

The beautiful Queen Helen was found. She and the other Greeks boarded their ships to return to their homeland. This was the end of the war between the Greeks and the Trojans.

USE YOUR IMAGINATION: *I will be a Trojan who has gotten tired and sleepy from too much celebrating. You be Ulysses quietly leaving the wooden horse. You and your soldiers quickly gain control of the city. Find Queen Helen. Now everyone get ready to sail for Greece.*

ULYSSES QUESTIONS

1. What do people mean if they say someone is trying to bring a Trojan horse?

_____

_____

_____

2. What animal shape might you have created if you were trying to bring in secret troops? Draw a picture of your animal.

LEGENDS

3. How would you disguise a gift for a person you love or like? Draw a picture or write a paragraph about your idea.

_____

_____

_____

WHO'S WHO

GREEK GODS AND GODDESSES

Zeus

MYTHS

The Greeks used stories about their gods to explain things that happened in the world around them concerning nature. The king of all gods was Zeus, and his home was Mount Olympus. Zeus was like humans in many ways. His wife was Hera, who was the goddess of women and marriage as well as the queen of gods. The gods and goddesses at times even married humans and became mothers and fathers of humans. The difference between humans and gods was death. Gods never died.

Hades

Hera

Poseidon

Almost all of the gods and goddesses were in Zeus' family. Zeus had two brothers — Poseidon, the god of the ocean, earthquakes and horses, and Hades, who was the god of the underworld and the dead. Demeter and Hestia were Zeus' sisters. Demeter was the goddess of nature and the harvest, and Hestia was the goddess of hearth and home.

Demeter

Hestia

Hera and Zeus had many sons and daughters. Hebe was the goddess of eternal youth. There were the twins — Apollo, who was the god of sun, music, arts, and medicine, and Artemis, who was the goddess of the moon and hunting. Athena was Zeus' favorite daughter, and she was the goddess of wisdom and the city.

Apollo

Athena

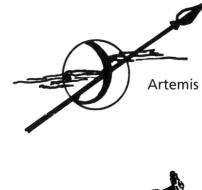

Artemis

Hephaestus

Another son, Hephaestus, was the god of fire, forge, and metal. Aphrodite was Hephaestus' wife and was the goddess of love and beauty. Aphrodite's son Eros was the god of love. His father was Ares, who was the god of war. Ares was Hephaestus' brother.

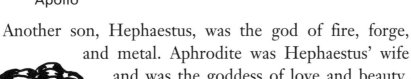

Aphrodite

Hermes was also Zeus' son and was the messenger of the gods. Dionysus was Zeus' youngest son and was the god of wine and wilderness.

Eros

Ares

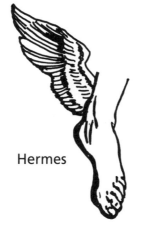

Hermes

Dionysus

49

GOD AND GODDESS MATCH-UP

____ 1. Aphrodite

____ 2. Apollo

____ 3. Ares

____ 4. Artemis

____ 5. Athena

____ 6. Demeter

____ 7. Dionysus

____ 8. Eros

____ 9. Hades

____10. Hephaestus

____11. Hera

____12. Hermes

____13. Hestia

____14. Poseidon

____15. Zeus

A. King of gods; god of sky and lightning

B. Queen of gods; goddess of women and marriage

C. God of the ocean, earthquakes, and horses

D. God of the underworld and the dead

E. God of the sun, music, arts, and medicine

F. Goddess of the moon and hunting

G. Goddess of wisdom and the city

H. Goddess of love and beauty

I. God of love

J. God of war

K. God of fire, forge, and metal

L. God of wine and wilderness

M. Messenger of the gods

N. Goddess of hearth and home

O. Goddess of nature and harvest

Athena

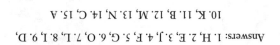
Answers: 1. H, 2. E, 3. J, 4. F, 5. G, 6. O, 7. L, 8. I, 9. D, 10. K, 11. B, 12. M, 13. N, 14. C, 15. A

MYTHS

WRITE YOUR OWN MYTH

Refer to the *Who's Who of Gods and Goddesses*. Find a book on Greek myths and read several of them. Next, write your own myth explaining some type of natural event.

MYTHS

Greek Gods and Goddesses

Zeus

MYTHS

Hera

WORD BOX

Aphrodite	Hephaestus
Apollo	Hera
Ares	Hermes
Artemis	Hestia
Athena	Poseidon
Demeter	Zeus
Dionysus	
Eros	
Hades	

Across

1. God of the sun, music, arts, and medicine
3. Messenger of the gods
7. Goddess of love and beauty
9. God of the underworld
10. Goddess of nature and the harvest
11. Goddess of hearth and home
12. God of war
13. King of gods; god of sky and lightning

Down

2. God of the ocean, earthquakes, and horses
4. God of love
5. Goddess of moon and hunting
6. God of wine and wilderness
7. Goddess of wisdom and the city
8. God of fire, forge, and metal
11. Queen of gods; goddess of women and marriage

EDUCATION OF MIND & BODY

OR HOW I GOT TO GO TO THE OLYMPICS

Plato

In ancient Greece, only boys went to school because only males could become voting citizens. The Greeks believed in living a balanced and harmonious life, which began with an education that developed both the mind and the body. According to Plato, this education was to help boys "be more gentle and harmonious and rhythmical, and so more fitted for speech and action; for the life of man in every part has need of harmony and rhythm."

This Greek philosophy and the schools both helped young boys to develop into athletic young men. During times of war or peace, the young Greeks were prepared both in body and mind. When there was no war, this physical training led many of them to the Olympic competitions in Olympia.

OLYMPICS

Greek Athletes

OLYMPICS: A RELIGIOUS FESTIVAL

Competing in the Olympics was a way for young Greeks to honor their gods. The first known Olympic games were held in 776 BC in Olympia as a religious festival to honor Zeus, the king of the gods. Mount Olympus was the legendary home of Zeus. The games were held every four years for a thousand years. For the first 13 of these Olympic games, foot races were the only games. The race was about 200 yards (180 meters) or about the length of two football fields.

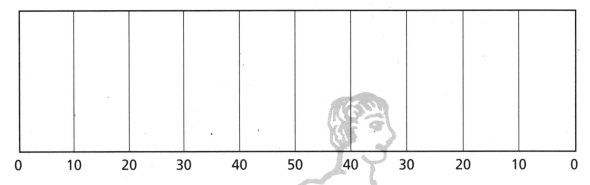

| 0 | 10 | 20 | 30 | 40 | 50 | 40 | 30 | 20 | 10 | 0 |

The games gave young men an opportunity to compete against other Greeks and demonstrate how well they had developed individual physical skills and abilities. The games gave the many, varied, individual Greek city-states a feeling of unity. As time passed, other competitions were added to the games including running, jumping, boxing, wrestling, chariot racing, javelin throwing, and discus throwing.

The Olympics were held every four years. Fill in the blanks below to tell approximately what year games other than foot races began? (Note: BC years get smaller in number as they move forward in time.)

1st OLYMPIC GAMES	776 BC
2nd	772 BC
3rd	768 BC
4th	764 BC
5th	760 BC
6th	756 BC
7th	752 BC
8th	748 BC
9th	744 BC
10th	740 BC
11th	736 BC
12th	732 BC
13th	728 BC
14th	724 BC

THE DISCUS THROWER BY MYRON

About 450 BC, the Greek sculptor Myron created the *Discus Thrower* in bronze. It is only known to us from Roman copies. The naturalness and grace of the athlete in this sculpture are a sharp contrast to the stiff and rigid portraits in Egyptian art. Greek sculpture looks natural and realistic, but it is also idealistic. The faces do not show flaws or individualistic traits.

Draw another face for the Discus Thrower that would not be an idealized face.

BALANCE OF MIND AND BODY

The *Discus Thrower* shows some of the ideals that Greeks such as Plato believed to be important. The statue shows a well-trained athlete who is in the process of throwing a discus. He is focused, confident, and in control of his mind and body. In addition to being a good athlete, this young man also would have had a good education for his mind. He would not be an ignorant athlete. There was balance between his mind and body. What other types of balance does the *Discus Thrower* show?

OLYMPICS

GREECE

WORD **BOX**

idealism
alertness
movement

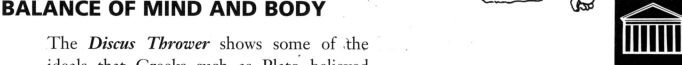

- A balance between realism and _____ .
- A balance between stillness and _____ .
- A balance between calmness and _____ .

ASYMMETRICAL BALANCE

In this sculpture you will see asymmetrical balance. This means that the sides do not match, but there is still balance. The sculpture does not fall over. The head balances the arm holding the discus while the bent legs balance the body.

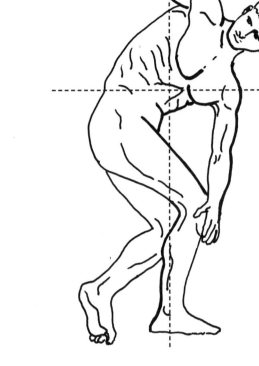

Make a list of many, varied, and unusual single words to describe the *Discus Thrower*. Use your own words or those from the IDEA BOX.

_____

_____

_____

_____

OLYMPICS

GREECE

IDEA BOX

harmonious	cool
moving	natural
focused	active
collected	balanced
calm	

Olympics

Refer to the Greek section on the Olympics for help in solving this puzzle.

GREECE

WORD LIST

balance	religious
boxing	rhythm
footraces	unity
harmony	wrestling
Myron	Zeus

OLYMPICS

Across

2. The first Olympic games were held as this kind of festival.
3. The **Discus Thrower** is said to show an athlete with _____ of mind and body.
4. The Olympic games gave individual Greek city-states a feeling of _____.
5. According to Plato, this is one of the two basic needs that man has for life.
8. The first Olympic games were created to honor this king of the gods.
9. Plato observed this as one of the two basic needs that man has for life.

Down

1. The only competition that was held in the first 13 Olympics.
3. One of the many competitions added to the original Olympic games.
6. The sculptor who created the **Discus Thrower** in bronze.
7. One of the many competitions added to the original Olympic games.

OLYMPIC TRAINING

Imagine that you are in training for the Olympics. Your trainer wants you to learn to check your pulse.

1. Run in place for one minute.

2. Find your pulse by placing your fingers (not thumbs) on your neck. Count your pulse as it slowly goes back to normal.

3. Run again in place for one minute. Notice what is happening to your heart beat.

4. Count your pulse rate using the pulse you found in your neck.

   What is your pulse rate immediately after running for one minute? _____

5. Rest until you feel your heart rate slowing to normal.

   What is your pulse rate now?_____

OLYMPICS

YOU ARE AN ATHLETE AT THE FIRST OLYMPICS

The year is 776 BC, and you are an athlete in the first Greek Olympics. In the stands are 40,000 spectators, watching, screaming, and cheering. The sun is piercing you from the blue sky as sweat pours down the sides of your cheeks. You are lined up at the starting point with all of the other men competing in a footrace. Suddenly the race starts, and you're off! Think about what you would have seen and what sounds you would have heard during this exciting race.
Fill those in on the chart below. Then imagine what you would feel with your fingers, toes, and skin. Write those ideas under the touch column. What could you have tasted or smelled in that place?

See	Hear	Touch	Smell	Taste

OLYMPICS

Now write a paragraph describing what it was like to be this Olympic athlete.

I am _____

_____

_____

_____

_____

_____

CREATE YOUR OWN DISCUS

The *Discus Thrower* by Myron is a beautiful example of an idealized figure that shows harmony and order. Imagine that you have been asked by the Olympic committee to invent a new and improved discus that will still exhibit the Greek virtues of nothing to excess, harmony, and order. Try these experiments. Design and create your own discus.

MATERIALS:

- 2 paper plates
- 2 plastic plates
- 2 styrofoam plates
- tape or stapler

Staple or tape 2 similar plates together top to top to form a discus shape. Which flies best? Record your observations.

	1ST TRIAL	2ND TRIAL	3RD TRIAL
Paper plate			
Styrofoam			
Plastic			

Draw and decorate a discus.

What happens if you add weight to your discus? Would the weight need to be evenly distributed? Record your experiments.

Materials used for weight:

_____

_____

	1ST TRIAL	2ND TRIAL	3RD TRIAL
Modified paper			
Modified styrofoam			
Modified plastic			

Now draw the trajectory (flight pattern) of your discus, using a dotted line.

OLYMPICS

YOU ARE AN OLYMPIC DISCUS THROWER

This is your first Olympic game. The year is 460 BC and you have been chosen to go to Olympia to compete in the discus throwing contest. You have just arrived but many other young and old men are already there. Many are worshipping in the sacred grove near the place where the Cladeus River flows into the Alpheus River. They want to see the newly restored Temple of Zeus. Other athletes are congregating near the athletic buildings.

The sun is hot overhead. You are carrying your discus and your food. Pebbles have just gotten in your sandals. What things will you be seeing and hearing? How will the weight of the discus and the aroma of the food affect you? How will your feet feel? Fill out the chart below by describing how your five senses are being affected by your environment.

See	Hear	Touch	Smell	Taste

OLYMPICS

Now write a poem describing what it was like to be an Olympic discus thrower.

_____

_____

_____

_____

_____

_____

Draw a picture of what you might have seen.

OLYMPICS

PYTHAGOREAN SCHOOL

Pythagoras was a Greek philosopher and mathematician who lived around 550 BC. His Pythagorean school motto was "All is number." Pythagoras established this school which was communal and secret. Its members were vegetarian, and all knowledge and property were held in common. Rituals in the Pythagorean School included the harmonies and mysteries of philosophy (love of wisdom) and mathematics.

A famous theorem was discovered by the Pythagoreans. In a right triangle where a and b are the legs and c is the hypotenuse, the Pythorgean Theorem states that

$$a^2 + b^2 = c^2$$

Three numbers that satisfy the theorem are called Pythagorean triples. 3-4-5 is a Pythagorean triple because $3^2 + 4^2 = 5^2$, or $9 + 16 = 25$.

Complete these Pythagorean triples:

1. 6–8–_____

2. 5–12–_____

3. 9–_____–15

Hint: $9^2 + x^2 = 15^2$ or $15^2 - 9^2 = x^2$

4. _____–15–17

5. 12–_____–20

6. _____–24–25

7. 30–_____–50

8. _____–80–100

Can you find any others?

PHILOSOPHY

THREE GREEK PHILOSOPHERS

Socrates

What is the meaning of life? What is happiness? These are questions that a philosopher asks. A philosopher is someone who thinks about the meaning of life and man's part in life. From ancient Greece came three famous philosophers whose ideas still influence us today. These three philosophers and teachers, Socrates, Plato, and Aristotle, learned from each other and sought truth for themselves. Their ideas greatly influenced Western culture.

Socrates: 469 BC - 399 BC

Socrates was the first of the three great Greek philosophers. He believed that people would always do good if they knew what "good" was. He believed that people lost happiness by choosing the wrong "good" things, such as wealth and power. Socrates felt it was his mission in life to make people think and to separate true knowledge from opinion.

Wearing no shoes and the same clothing year round, Socrates carried out his mission in life by giving up any form of money making. He spent his life in the marketplace and the streets of Athens talking to people and helping them to know themselves. He asked his fellow Athenians questions such as:

What is justice?

What is beauty?

What is friendship?

PHILOSOPHY

Socrates listened to the answers people gave to his questions. He tried to make people think. He enjoyed helping them to see the errors of their thinking. He considered himself to be like "a fly who must sting a lazy horse." As you might imagine, however, some people didn't like him. Some Athenians did not particularly enjoy having their thoughts criticized. He made many enemies which eventually led to his trial and death. In 399 BC, he was put on trial for putting "dangerous" ideas into the heads of young people and sentenced to death. He was ordered to drink poisonous hemlock.

Socrates left no written information about his philosophy of life and man. We know about his teachings only through his student, Plato, the next important Greek philosopher.

INTERACTIONS

Ask three or more people the questions below. Record their responses. Now add your own answers. Share them with someone.

    1. What is goodness?

_____
_____
_____

    2. What is beauty?

_____
_____
_____

    3. What is virtue?

_____
_____
_____

    4. What is justice?

_____
_____
_____

    5. What is friendship?

PHILOSOPHY

_____
_____
_____

EXTENSION

Write your own philosophical questions to ask others.

_____
_____
_____
_____
_____
_____

DO THE IDEAS OF SOCRATES SEEM ABSTRACT?

LET'S MAKE THEM MORE SPECIFIC

Socrates thought in depth about such abstract ideas as beauty, truth, and justice. Pick one of these abstract ideas and write it on the line below.

My topic: _____

1. What animal is this topic like and why?

Animal: _____

_____

_____

_____

PHILOSOPHY

2. What plant is this topic like and why?

Plant: _____

_____

_____

_____

3. What shape is this topic like and why?

Shape: _____

_____

_____

_____

4. What color is this topic like and why?

Color: _____

_____

_____

_____

5. Now pick your favorite description—either animal, plant, shape, or color. Pick more words that complete this description.

My favorite: _____

Nouns - add person, place, or thing words

_____   _____   _____

Verbs - add action or being words

_____   _____   _____

Adjectives - add words to describe your nouns

_____   _____   _____

PHILOSOPHY

6. Now use your ideas to write a short, specific poem to describe this idea.

My abstract idea: _____

_____

_____

_____

_____

_____

_____

_____

_____

_____

_____

_____

_____

_____

PHILOSOPHY

PLATO
427 BC–347 BC

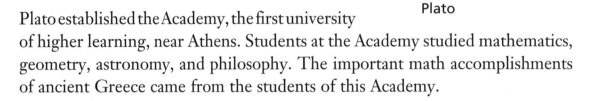
Plato

The Greek philosopher Plato was a student and friend of Socrates. It is from the writings of Plato that we know about Socrates. Plato's early writings were of conversations between himself and Socrates in which they discussed Socrates' view of the world.

Plato established the Academy, the first university of higher learning, near Athens. Students at the Academy studied mathematics, geometry, astronomy, and philosophy. The important math accomplishments of ancient Greece came from the students of this Academy.

Plato divided man's soul into three parts: the rational and reasoning part of man, his desires or appetites, and his spirit or will. He said that the most noble of these three was the rational part of man. He believed that harmony occurred when reason controlled man rather than his appetites or will.

Plato felt that each man should be tested on the basis of his education and given a rank (not based on birth or wealth) in society according to which part of his soul was in charge of the man. If a man's reasoning was in charge, he should be a politician. Men whose appetites were in charge should deal in business. Those whose wills were in charge should be in the police or military.

PHILOSOPHY

Many of Plato's ideas centered around what type of government would be the best. He believed that philosophers were the only ones who were qualified to be leaders because only they truly understood justice. He thought leaders should study arithmetic, plane and solid geometry, astronomy, and harmonics for 10 years. This should be followed by five years of dialectic study, the art of asking important questions and answering them accurately according to appropriate verbal reasoning.

Aristotle, Plato's most famous student at the Academy, said that Plato was so noble that bad men should not even speak his name.

GREAT LEADERS

Think of great leaders in history. What are some of the characteristics that made them good leaders? Were they fair? Were they honest?

Pericles

1. List 10 qualities that you believe make a good leader.

   _____   _____

   _____   _____

   _____   _____

   _____   _____

   _____   _____

2. List 10 qualities that you believe make a poor leader.

   _____   _____

   _____   _____

   _____   _____

   _____   _____

   _____   _____

PHILOSOPHY

3. Make a list of people you know personally who are leaders. They may be your parents, your principal, your teachers, your classmates or your friends.

   _____

   _____

   _____

   _____

   _____

ARISTOTLE

Aristotle

Aristotle is known as "the father of scientific method." While teaching at the Lyceum, he explained that everything had a place in the world scheme. He thought every person should understand physics because it defined nature and the purpose of things.

Aristotle used syllogisms as a method of reasoning. A syllogism is a conclusion based on two related true statements. For example:

1. All mammals have hair or fur.
2. A cat has fur.
3. Therefore, a cat is a mammal.

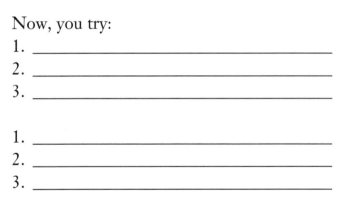

1. All smooth, round objects roll.
2. A ball rolls.
3. Therefore, a ball is a smooth, round object.

Now, you try:
1. _____
2. _____
3. _____

1. _____
2. _____
3. _____

PHILOSOPHY

Aristotle classified over 500 animals, made careful observations on developing chicks, and compared human and animal structures like fingernails and claws, or hands and front paws.

Can you think of other similarities?

1. Human hair and _____
2. Human feet and _____
3. _____
4. _____
5. _____

GREECE

SCIENCE

HIPPOCRATES

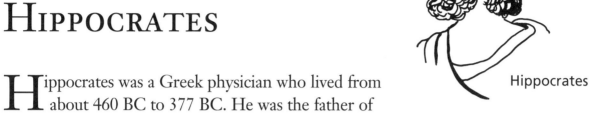

Hippocrates

Hippocrates was a Greek physician who lived from about 460 BC to 377 BC. He was the father of medicine and made careful observations and recordings of factual information. The Hippocratic Oath has been a guide for physicians for more than 2,000 years. When taking this oath, a physician promises to keep what patients tell him or her private, to protect life, to try to treat diseases, and to be honest. In the days of Hippocrates, remedies were usually rest and changes in the diet. There were not many medicines, although herbs were used to treat patients. Today we know many of the herbs actually contained real medicine.

Hippocrates observed balance and symmetry in the human body. What balance or symmetry can you observe?

RIGHT SIDE   LEFT SIDE

1. one eye   the other eye
2. five fingers   _____
3. _____   _____
4. _____   _____
5. _____   _____

Carefully observe your hand, finger, and fingernail. Draw what you see. Compare your hand to the hand of someone else. How are they alike or different?

SCIENCE

YOUR HAND   SOMEONE ELSE'S HAND

73

ARCHIMEDES AND THE KING'S CROWN

Circa (about) 287–212 BC

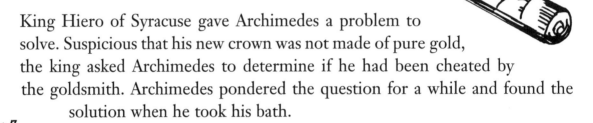
Archimedes

Archimedes was a famous Greek mathematician and inventor. He is credited with discovering the principles of the lever and inventing the movable pulley. One of his inventions, the hydraulic screw, was designed to move water uphill. The hydraulic screw is still used today to move all kinds of things. If you have an icemaker in your freezer, you can see Archimedes' famous screw at work moving your ice.

King Hiero of Syracuse gave Archimedes a problem to solve. Suspicious that his new crown was not made of pure gold, the king asked Archimedes to determine if he had been cheated by the goldsmith. Archimedes pondered the question for a while and found the solution when he took his bath.

The bathtub had been filled to the brim, and when Archimedes stepped into the water, much of the water sloshed onto the floor. He then reasoned that a crown of pure gold should displace or move as much water as an ingot of pure gold weighing as much as the crown. He was so excited by this discovery that he ran naked into the street shouting "Eureka!" This is Greek for "I found it!" One can only suspect that his neighbors were as surprised by this discovery as Archimedes.

After apologizing to the neighbors and dressing himself properly, Archimedes tested the king's crown. King Hiero's suspicions were well founded — the crown was not made of pure gold. The goldsmith had cheated the king, and Archimedes' reputation as an odd, yet intelligent man was secured.

SCIENCE

Activity~

Fill a glass half full of water. Slowly add coins and watch how the level of the water rises.

LET'S ORGANIZE JUMBLED IDEAS ABOUT ARCHIMEDES

Below is a collection of facts about Archimedes, a Greek inventor and mathematician. They are in no particular order. As you read these facts, think about how you would group them into categories.

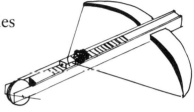

1. He is best known as the inventor of the Archimedes screw.

2. He is called the greatest engineer of the classical age.

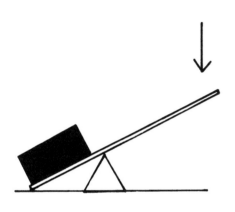

3. He also invented the catapult, a weapon used in war to shoot rocks.

4. He was born around 300 BC in the Greek city-state of Syracuse. As a young boy he probably studied in Alexandria, Egypt.

5. He also discovered why a lever and a pulley work. These two simple machines led to the construction of machines that could move heavy loads.

6. The lever is a simple machine used for performing work. It helps lift weights with less effort.

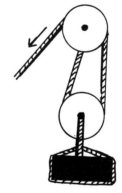

7. A pulley is another simple machine used for performing work. A pulley makes lifting loads easier because it uses a wheel with a rope or belt running over the top. A person can use body weight to pull down on the rope. This body weight turns the wheel and lifts the load on the other side.

SCIENCE

8. The Archimedean screw is still used today to lift water for irrigation.

9. He is also credited with designing a system of mirrors that would focus the sun's rays. These were used in fighting to start fires on enemy ships.

10. He is a Greek mathematician and inventor who made some basic scientific discoveries.

11. Archimedes was killed in 212 BC when the Romans captured Syracuse. The Roman soldiers were told not to hurt Archimedes. However, legend claims that a soldier did not recognize him and stabbed him with a sword while he was drawing geometric figures in the sand.

12. The Archimedean screw is a very large screw that fits tightly inside a cylindrical case. One end is lowered into water, and the screw is tilted up on a slant. The upper end has a handle which turns the screw. As the handle turns, water is raised upward inside the screw until it pours out the upper end.

13. Some people call Archimedes the "father of experimental science" because he didn't just think about ideas. He also tested them with experiments to see if they worked.

14. To Archimedes inventing was the same as playing.

* * * * *

SCIENCE

On the next page you will web these ideas about Archimedes into categories. A web is a graphic organizer that visually allows students to see how facts group together by topic.

As you try to think of categories for these facts, think about Archimedes' life, his main invention, and Archimedes' other inventions.

WEB OF ARCHIMEDES

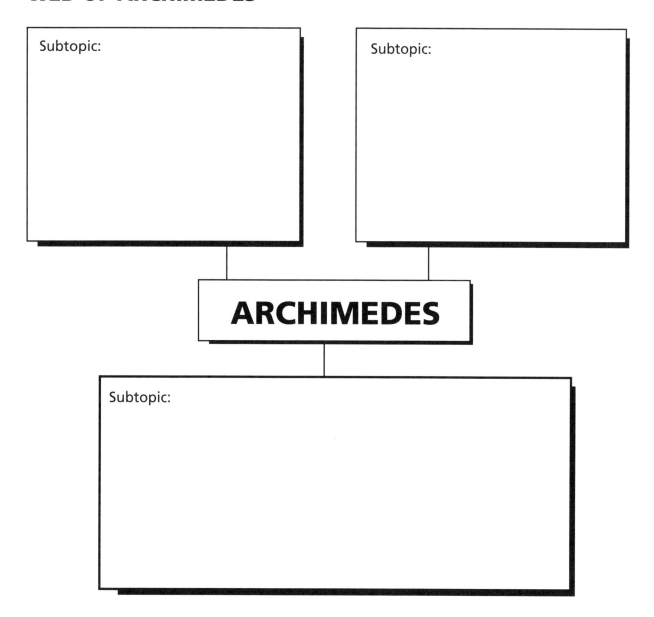

Subtopic:

Subtopic:

ARCHIMEDES

Subtopic:

INSTRUCTIONS

1. The name Archimedes is placed in the middle rectangle. This is the main topic of your web.

2. In the three rectangles attached to the middle main topic, write the three main categories of facts about Archimedes from the facts on the previous pages. These three rectangles are called the subtopics of your webs.

3. Add details from the facts on the previous pages. Be sure they are attached to the matching subtopic rectangle. These are called the supporting details of your web.

SCIENCE

ARCHIMEDES SHORT STORY

Use the web to write a short story about Archimedes and illustrate it.

THE STORY OF ARCHIMEDES

_____

_____

_____

_____

_____

_____

_____

_____

SCIENCE

ARCHIMEDES SIMPLE EXPERIMENTS

Archimedes was the first person to scientifically study the simple machines.

1. **Lever** - can be used to lift or pull a load.
2. **Wedge** - helps you cut, split, or push something.
3. **Inclined plane** - can be used to move things easily and smoothly.
4. **Wheel and axle** - can be used to move a load. The axle is the rod that runs through the wheels and helps them turn.
5. **Pulley** - can be used to move things up and down. It is made from a rope and a wheel with a groove.
6. **Screw** - can hold things together or raise and lower things.

What simple machine is involved in each picture below? Write the name on the line provided.

Wagon

Slide

_____

_____

_____

_____

Saw

Clamp

_____

_____

_____

_____

Flag pole

See-Saw

_____

_____

_____

_____

SCIENCE

79

ARCHIMEDES: EXPERIMENTS

Although even primitive peoples used the lever, Archimedes developed the formal mathematical principles of levers and pulleys. According to stories handed down over time, he moved a loaded ship from the harbor to the sand, by himself, using a series of pulleys. Levers and pulleys are simple machines.

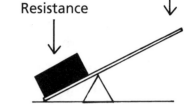

The Lever. Using a bar and a fulcrum, you can discover some things about levers and physics. Two important words to learn are **resistance** and **effort**.

Resistance is a weight to be moved, and effort is the force (made by another weight) needed to move the resistance.

Experiment: Use a 12-inch ruler for the bar, three old markers taped together for a fulcrum, and two paper cups taped to the ruler. Put your resistance in one cup and your effort in the other (suggestion: use pennies for resistance and effort). The fulcrum should be at the 6-inch mark. Try using six pennies as your resistance.

Tape the cup holding the resistance at the 1-inch mark. Tape the cup to hold the effort at the other end of the ruler. How many pennies must you put in the effort cup to lift your resistance? Now put the fulcrum at the 6-inch mark. How many pennies does it take now to lift the resistance?

Move your fulcrum an inch at a time.
Record your results:

SCIENCE

FULCRUM	PENNIES NEEDED
5 inches	
4 inches	
3 inches	
8 inches	
9 inches	

What did you discover? For more exciting experiments, try using different numbers of pennies for your resistance.

ARCHIMEDES' SCREW

One of Archimedes' most important and usable inventions was the Archimedean screw, which could bring water from a lower to a higher level. An Archimedean screw is a spiral shape inside a cylinder. As the screw is turned, water is carried upward. Today you can find a similar device in an icemaker that delivers ice through the door of a freezer.

BUOYANCE AND SPECIFIC GRAVITY

Archimedes was the first person to develop the idea that explains buoyancy and specific gravity.

EXPERIMENT:

Put an equal amount of water in two jars and mark the water level. Put 20 pennies in each jar and mark the level again. What happened?

Now put an equal amount of water in two jars again and mark the water level. This time put 10 pennies in one and 25 in the other, and mark the water levels. What happened?

_____

_____

Did your results surprise you? Why?

_____

_____

Start out again with your two jars with equal amounts of water. Mark your water levels. Now put a few marbles in one jar and mark the new water level. Make the same number of balls out of Play-Doh™. What do you think will happen when you put them in the second jar?

Now try it and record your observations.

_____

_____

What else could you try?

_____

_____

Use your imagination and draw pictures of things you would like to make or build.

SCIENCE

GREECE
REVIEW

ATHENS DAY

FOOD

In celebration of your study of ancient Greece, have an Athens Day. Eat foods commonly eaten in ancient Greece such as pomegranate, olives, and pita bread.

TABLETS

Since students in ancient Greece wrote on wax tablets instead of paper, make a wax tablet by covering a piece of cardboard with a layer of crayon (any color). Simply take your crayons and color very heavily with them. Next, add a layer of black crayon. Then write on the "tablets" using a sharp object such as a straightened paper clip or a stick.

GAME

You can also play a game that was played in ancient Greece called knucklebones. In Greece it was played using the knucklebones of sheep. You may substitute paper mache pieces shaped like bones. To play the game, throw the "bones" into the air and try to catch them on your knuckles. It is a game very much like "Jacks."

CLOTHING

Greek clothing was very simple. The clothes were draped around their bodies rather than fitted. Only the rich wore brightly colored clothes. As part of your celebration, dress as the Greeks would have dressed. You might be able to use a white sheet or tablecloth to drape around you.

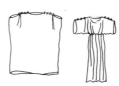

| Peplos | Chiton | Mantle | Peplos over Chiton | Mantle |

HEAD DRESS

If you wish to imagine yourself as an Olympic winner, you might make yourself a crown of ivy leaves.

REVIEW

CLASSICAL GREECE

In this unit you have learned about artists and their artwork, inventors and their inventions as well as famous architecture built during this era. Use your productive thinking skills to choose:

1. One of my favorite simple machines is the

   _____ .

   It can be used to _____ .

2. One of my favorite people from ancient Greece is _____

   _____ .

   This artist is famous for _____ .

3. A work of architecture I learned about was _____

   _____ .

   It is located in _____ .

   Some of its features are _____

   _____ .

4. A famous mythological person from this period is

   _____ .

   That person is famous for_____ .

5. If I had lived in the Classical Greek time I would have been a

   _____and_____ .

84

IDENTIFY THE FOLLOWING:

_____

_____

_____   _____   _____

LETTER HOME FROM GREECE

Now that you have completed your imaginary trip to ancient Greece, write a letter home. Tell about the important ideas, people, and things you learned.

Letter from _____

After My Travels to Classical Greece

Date: _____

Dear _____ ,

_____

_____

_____

_____

_____

_____

_____

_____

_____

Bibliography

Antoniou, Jim. *Cities Then and Now*. Macmillan.

Cole, Bruce and Adelheid Gelat. *Art of the Western World*. Summit Books.

Dorra, Henri. *Art in Perspective*. Harcourt Brace Jovanovich.

Foster, Genevieve. *Augustus Caesar's World*. Charles Scribner's Sons.

Hodges, Henry. *Technology in the Ancient World*. Barnes and Noble.

James, Peter and Nick Thorpe. *Ancient Inventions*. Ballantine Books.

Janson, H.W. *History of Art*. Prentice Hall.

Langen, Annette. *Felix Travels Back in Time*. Abbeville.

Low, Alice. *Macmillan Book of Greek Gods and Heroes*. Macmillan.

Pearson, Ann. *Ancient Greece*. Alfred Knopf.

Pedley, John. *Greek Art and Archaelogy*. Prentice Hall.

Platt, Richard. *Smithsonian Visual Timeline of Inventions*. Dorling Kindersley.

Steves, Rick and Gene Openshaw. *Europe 101*. John Muir Publications.

Strickland, Carol and John Boswell. *The Annotated Mona Lisa*. Universal.

Turvey, Peter. *Timelines Inventions*. Franklin Watts.

Winters, Nathan. *Architecture is Elementary*. Gibbs Smith Publisher.